Noah's Park

DREAMER AND THE MYSTERY OF COZY CAVE

Written by Richard Hays
Illustrated by Chris Sharp

A Faith Parenting Guide can be found on |

D1401927

Faith Kids®
is an imprint of Cook Communications Ministries,
Colorado Springs, Colorado 80918
Cook Communications, Paris, Ontario
Kingsway Communications, Eastbourne, England

DREAMER AND THE MYSTERY OF COZY CAVE
©2000 by The Illustrated Word, Inc.

First printing, 2000
Printed in Canada
04 03 02 01 00   5 4 3 2 1

Digital art and design: Gary Currant
Executive Producer: Kenneth R. Wilcox

Dreamer and the Mystery of Cozy Cave

My child's need: To learn what it means to have courage.

Biblical value: Courage

Learning styles: Help your child to realize more about the courage and trust that comes from God in the following ways:

Sight: Go through the book and find those characters that look scared. Why do they look scared? What happens to us when we feel afraid? How can God help us to feel better? Where does Dreamer learn to have more courage? Reread that portion of the story.

Sound: Read the story aloud with your child. Think about a time when you or your child felt frightened about something. Talk about how you handled it. What helped you to feel better? Talk about how sometimes just the darkness of the night can make sounds and sights seem more scary. Where is God when we're in the dark?

Touch: Play a game with your child. Turn out the lights and give things to your child to touch and describe how the objects feel. If possible, have some of your choices be some cut up watermelon, some grapes, and some spaghetti. Ask your child what he imagines each thing to be. Ask if your child can understand how Dreamer became afraid? Turn on the lights and show the objects. Say a prayer together that God will always give you courage in the dark or the light.

Dreamer looked out from Cozy Cave and watched the orange sun setting over Noah's Park. The rhinoceros yawned. He was very tired. All day he and his friends had been eating a new crop of watermelons that had suddenly popped up all over the park. The watermelons were delicious, but all the eating had kept Dreamer from taking his normal three naps.

Dreamer put his head down on the warm sand. He was asleep before he counted even one sheep. Dreamer loved to dream, and he was soon dreaming again. In his dream he sat down on a rock and leaned back against the cave wall. He heard a *pop, pop, pop!* Green smoke puffed out across the cave. When the smoke cleared, there was an open door. Through the opening, Dreamer saw a funny green glow. He decided to see where the glow was coming from, but as he took his first step, he woke up.

The next morning Dreamer told Honk the camel and Ponder the frog about his dream. "It was so real," the rhino told them.

Ponder and Honk smiled at each other. They had heard this before. "It was just a dream," said Honk, who was brushing his teeth. "You probably ate too many melons. That would explain that green glow."

"Remember that God is watching out for you when you sleep, too, Dreamer," Ponder added.

The next night Dreamer had
the dream again, but
this time he did not
wake up as he started
to go through the door.
He looked both ways and
took his first step.
"Whoa!" he yelled as he began
to slip, then fall, then slide.
"Look out below!"
he yelled as he slid
down and around
right into Polka Dot Pond.

He woke up shivering.
What happened? he wondered.
He was lying in Cozy Cave,
and he was all wet!

"How could I be wet?" Dreamer asked his friends the next morning. "The water isn't supposed to be real in a dream."

Screech the monkey and Shadow the raccoon laughed.

"You were probably sleep-walking and fell into the pond again." Shadow grinned.

"No, that's not right, Shadow. I'm sure that there is a secret door in Cozy Cave, and I'm going to find it." Dreamer turned and waddled toward the cave.

"Wait, Dreamer," said Honk with a sigh. "I'll go with you."

"So will I, Dreamer," said Ponder. "But if we are to have an adventure, first we must prepare."

"We'll all help," said the others.

The animals spent the next few days getting ready for their adventure. Everyone wanted to go, but Ponder decided that if they found the passage, Dreamer, Honk, Screech, and he would explore it.

"You're too tall, Stretch," Ponder explained, "and, well, you're too... er... wide, Ivory."

Finally, they were ready to start. They all gathered in Cozy Cave.

"Just do what you did in the dream," Ponder told the rhino. Dreamer nodded and started going from rock to rock. He sat on each one. Nothing happened. Then he started jumping on the rocks. Still no door appeared.

"Maybe it was not a rock that opened the door," Ponder said. "What else did you do, Dreamer, before the door opened?"

"Nothing much," said the rhino. "I just leaned back against the wall. Like this." There was a *pop, pop, pop*, a puff of green smoke, and the door appeared.

Dreamer crossed to the door and peeked into the passage. He saw a green glow, just as he did in his dream. He took a step to go in, but then stopped. The others, following close behind, piled into him.

"What's wrong, Dreamer?" Ponder asked.

"I'm scared," said Dreamer. "It was okay to be a brave adventurer in my dream, but this is different. We don't know what's down there. It could be very dangerous."

Ponder looked at him and the others. "When we started, I did not believe there was a secret door. I was wrong. Now we must explore these passages to make sure there is nothing to threaten our home. We must know the secret of Cozy Cave. Dreamer, remember the stories I have told you about Noah. He was frightened, too, when God told him to build the ark and save the animals. God gave Noah the courage to follow His will. God will give you, Dreamer, the courage to lead us now."

Dreamer looked at the frog. He nodded his large head.

"I will go." He entered the door. Their adventure had begun.

Dreamer, Ponder, Honk, and Screech followed the green glow for what seemed like days. They traveled deep into the earth and then climbed back up. They crossed underground rivers and dodged rolling boulders.

Dreamer lost his courage many
times during the journey, and Ponder, Honk, and
Screech each saved the rhino from the dangers of the cave.
Each time, though, Dreamer found the courage to lead them forward.

Finally, they came to a huge open cavern.
In the middle of the cavern was a lake,
and in the middle of the lake was an island.
The island was the source of the green glow
they had been following. The animals had
reached the end of their journey.
"What do we do now?" Screech asked.

"I think we need to find out what is on that island," Honk said, "but I don't want to swim across the lake to get there. Of course, we could all use a bath..."

"You can take a bath if you want, Honk," Dreamer told the camel. "The rest of us can go to the island in this boat." Dreamer pulled a small rowboat from behind a rock.

He pushed it into the water and climbed aboard. The others laughed and scrambled into the boat too.

Dreamer and Honk used the two oars to row across the lake. Soon the friends were standing on the island's sandy beach. They could now see that the island was covered with white and yellow flowers. In the middle of the island was a strange-looking hill. Green fog swirled around it.

"Look at the flowers!" Screech yelled. He leaped forward and began rolling around in the flower field. Honk and Ponder joined him. Dreamer did not move. He just stood on the beach and stared at the fog-covered hill.

"Hey, the flowers are connected by vines," said Screech, "but they smell good enough to eat. Come on, Dreamer."

Dreamer still did not move. As he watched,
the fog began to clear. The shape of the hill seemed
familiar. Suddenly, the rhino realized that the hill was
not a hill at all. It was a giant watermelon, and it had
just opened its eyes. It was alive!

Dreamer took out the wooden whistle Howler had made and blew it loudly. Ponder, Screech, and Honk looked up. They saw the watermelon. Before they could move, though, the flower vines reached out and grabbed them. The vines were the arms of the watermelon! The watermelon opened its mouth and grinned a jack-o'-lantern grin.

"Help, Dreamer," yelled Honk. "I've been camelnapped by a fruit!"

"Isn't a watermelon a vegetable?" asked Screech.

"Who cares!" screamed the camel as the vines lifted his friends high into the air. "This thing is about to eat us!"

Dreamer now saw that the watermelon had its mouth wide open and was indeed going to eat his friends.

"You have to help us, Dreamer!" Ponder called. "You are the only one who can save us!"

The rhinoceros began to shake. Sweat rolled down his face.

It is up to me! Dreamer thought. *Only I can save my friends.*

"You must have faith that God will give you the courage," yelled Ponder. "He will give you the courage you need!"

The watermelon laughed and began to lower the animals to its mouth. Dreamer closed his eyes for a moment. *Ponder is right,* he thought. *God will give me the courage!*

The rhinoceros lowered his head and charged the giant watermelon. Dozens of vines reached out to stop him, but Dreamer shook them off and ran even faster. The sleepy Dreamer was suddenly a powerful rhinoceros.

Dreamer slammed into the watermelon and the giant fruit exploded. Ponder, Screech, and Honk flew into the air and landed in the water. Dreamer splashed down beside them. Seeds and watermelon juice rained down on top of them.

"Dreamer," they all cheered. "Dreamer! Dreamer!"

"Dreamer! Dreamer! Wake up. You're dreaming."

The rhinoceros opened his eyes. Ponder, Screech, Honk, and all his other friends were gathered around him. He was lying in Cozy Cave, not splashing in the lake.

"Dreaming? It was just a dream?" Dreamer asked.

"You were yelling in your sleep. Something about watermelons," answered Honk. "Did you want some more?" The camel offered him a big slice of watermelon.

"No, no!" yelled Dreamer. "I never want to see a watermelon again." Then the rhino told them about his dream. When he was finished, all the animals were laughing, except Ponder.

"Well, Dreamer, even though it was just a dream, I think you should remember what you learned about trusting God to have courage. Sometimes God has funny ways of teaching us. I think you learned a very important lesson."

Later that night, Dreamer rested in Cozy Cave once more. He smiled as he remembered what Ponder had said. Ponder was certainly right about the lesson he had learned, but what a silly dream. Nothing so silly could ever happen.

Dreamer put his head down on the warm sand. He closed his eyes and luckily did not notice the puff of green smoke in the back of the cave.

DREAMER HAS A NIGHTMARE

Dreamer the rhinoceros loves to dream, until one day he has his first nightmare. How will Dreamer handle this frightening experience? Discover the answer in the Noah's Park adventure, *Dreamer Has a Nightmare*.

STRETCH'S TREASURE HUNT

Stretch the giraffe grew up watching her parents search for the Treasure of Nosy Rock. Imagine what happens when she finds out that the treasure might be buried in Noah's Park. Watch the fur fly as Stretch and her friends look for treasure in *Stretch's Treasure Hunt*.

CAMELS DON'T FLY

Honk the camel finds a statue of a camel with wings. Now, he is convinced that he can fly, too. Will Honk be the first camel to fly? Find out in the Noah's Park adventure, *Camels Don't Fly*.

HONK'S BIG ADVENTURE

On the first day of spring, all the animals of Noah's Park are playing in the mud, water, and leaves. This good clean fun creates a lot of dirty animals. When Honk the camel sees the mess, he decides to leave Noah's Park and find a clean place to live. Will Honk find what he searches for? Find out in the hilarious Noah's Park story, *Honk's Big Adventure*.

PONDER MEETS THE POLKA DOTS

Ponder the frog is growing lily pads in the Noah's Park pond. When something starts eating the lily pads, the normally calm frog decides to get even. Will Ponder save his lily pads? Find out in the colorful Noah's Park adventure, *Ponder Meets the Polka Dots*.